# As I Have Loved You

# As I Have Loved You

## Activity Ideas for Children

Written by Christena C. Nelson

Illustrated by Brenda Sorensen Braun

Deseret Book Company
Salt Lake City, Utah

To Laurie W. Thornton (1952–1995)
Thank you for all that you and Scott taught us about love unfeigned.

© 1995 Deseret Book Company

All rights reserved.
Individual illustrations may be reproduced for use in the classroom or at home.
For other use of book or any part herein, please contact the publisher,
Deseret Book Company, P. O. Box 30178, Salt Lake City, Utah 84130.
Whenever possible please include a credit line indicating the author, title, and publisher.
The reproduction of this book in whole is prohibited.

Deseret Book is a registered trademark of Deseret Book Company.

ISBN 1-57345-092-8

Printed in the United States of America
10   9   8   7   6   5   4   3   2

# Contents

Preface . . . . . . . . . . . . . . . . . . . . . . . . . . . . vii
1. The Love of God . . . . . . . . . . . . . . . . . . . . . . .1
2. Love Is Unconditional . . . . . . . . . . . . . . . . . . .7
3. Love Is for All . . . . . . . . . . . . . . . . . . . . . . . . 13
4. Love Does Not Judge Unrighteously . . . . . . . . . . . 16
5. Love Is Humility . . . . . . . . . . . . . . . . . . . . . . 19
6. Love Is Obedience to God . . . . . . . . . . . . . . . . 23
7. Love Is Forgiveness . . . . . . . . . . . . . . . . . . . . 28
8. Love Is Patience . . . . . . . . . . . . . . . . . . . . . . 31
9. Love Is Sharing . . . . . . . . . . . . . . . . . . . . . . 34
10. Love Is Sacrifice . . . . . . . . . . . . . . . . . . . . . . 36
11. Prayer Teaches Love . . . . . . . . . . . . . . . . . . . 40
12. The Scriptures Teach Love . . . . . . . . . . . . . . . 47
13. The Spirit Prompts Us to Love . . . . . . . . . . . . . 48
14. Priesthood Ordinances Increase Our Love . . . . . . 52
15. Love for Ourselves . . . . . . . . . . . . . . . . . . . . 57
16. Love for Our Families . . . . . . . . . . . . . . . . . . 60
17. Love for Our Friends and Neighbors . . . . . . . . . . 65
18. Love for the Whole World . . . . . . . . . . . . . . . . 70

# Preface

"As I have loved you, love one another." Just before the Savior's death, he taught his disciples this timeless truth: that love would be the identifying feature of those who served him. The Primary sacrament meeting presentation for 1996 is based on this important scripture.

How can we cultivate children's natural talent for loving others? How can we teach them to serve, to expand their love, to understand what love is?

*As I Have Loved You* was created to help teach children the principles and sources of love. The easy-to-prepare lesson activities are appropriate for Primary sharing times and classes, family home evenings, and other teaching moments.

You may photocopy, trace, enlarge, or reproduce the materials in this book for personal use at home or in the classroom (not for distribution). Many of the ideas could be presented effectively by older children. For ease of use in a family situation, you may wish to photocopy all the illustrations at once and keep them in a file, so a child could pick from the lessons when desired.

Feel free to use your creativity in adapting these materials to your own needs. We hope you will find them to be a valuable resource for teaching the most important topic of all: love.

# 1
# The Love of God

Love one another; as I have loved you.
(John 13:34)

**PREPARATION:** Cut a large heart puzzle from poster board. (See diagram.) Photocopy the picture of Jesus and the six smaller pictures. Leave the picture of Jesus black and white. Color and cut out the six small pictures and glue each to a puzzle piece. Slip the puzzle pieces into sections of folded newspaper, and stack the sections in numerical order. Glue the picture of Jesus to a section of newspaper and place it on the stack. Put a front-page section of newspaper on the top. Gather masking tape, a large flannel board, and an easel. Set the flannel board on the easel. Set the newspaper stack on a table.

**LESSON:** (Hold up the front-page section of newspaper.) What is this? What is a newspaper for? A newspaper is a report of what is happening. Sometimes the information is very sad. But today I have some good news. (Hold up the section with the picture of Jesus.) The good news is that we have a Savior who loves us. Let's look inside for more information.

One at a time, call on children to remove the puzzle pieces from the newspaper sections. Tape the pieces to the flannel board. Then discuss each picture. When the heart puzzle is complete, emphasize that everything the Savior does, he does out of love. If we want to be like he is, we will have to learn how to love as he does. Have the children repeat the scripture printed at the beginning of this chapter. Then go through each puzzle piece again. This time, discuss ways that *we* can show love as Jesus did. (Some ideas are given below.)

(Once again, hold up the newspaper section with the picture of Jesus.) What is the good news? We have a loving Savior! We can learn to love as he does.

Puzzle pieces:
1. *Jesus created the earth for us.*
He gave us everything we would need for clothes, food, shelter, and beauty.
We can care for all forms of life and give them what they need. We can create beautiful, uplifting things.
2. *Jesus taught the gospel.*
Christ's words are recorded in the scriptures.
We can teach others the gospel, after we study his words.
3. *Jesus gave us ordinances.*
Jesus gave us priesthood ordinances that, when honored, increase our love.
We can honor the priesthood by making and keeping covenants and by preparing to go to the temple.
4. *Jesus' life was a perfect example.*
Jesus never gave in to worldly temptations.

With the Lord's help, we can resist temptation. We can lead people to Christ, who is the only perfect example.

5. *Jesus suffered for us.*

Jesus suffered for our sins and afflictions, so he knows how to help us.

Our own pains and struggles can help us understand others who are suffering.

6. *Jesus died and was resurrected so we could all live again.*

Jesus is the only one who had the power to give up his life and take it back again. He gave up his life only when he had finished the work his Father had given him.

We can finish the work that Heavenly Father has sent us to do.

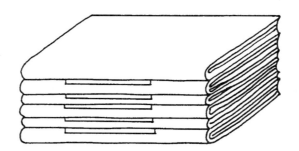

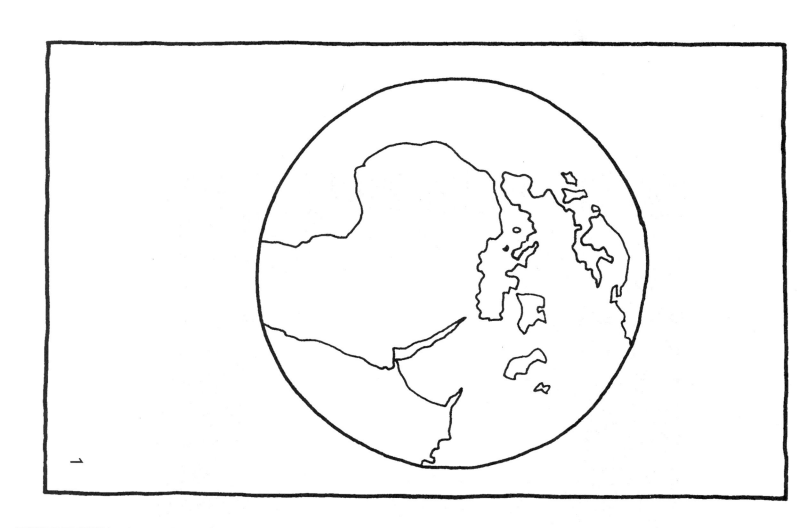
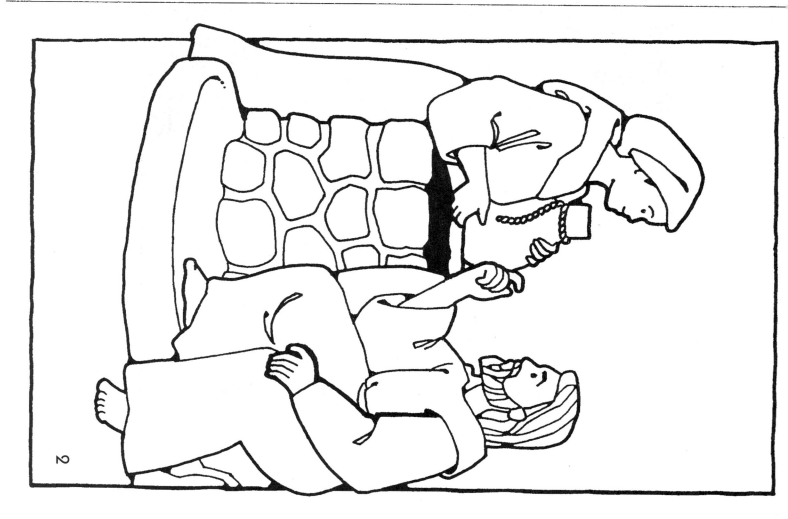

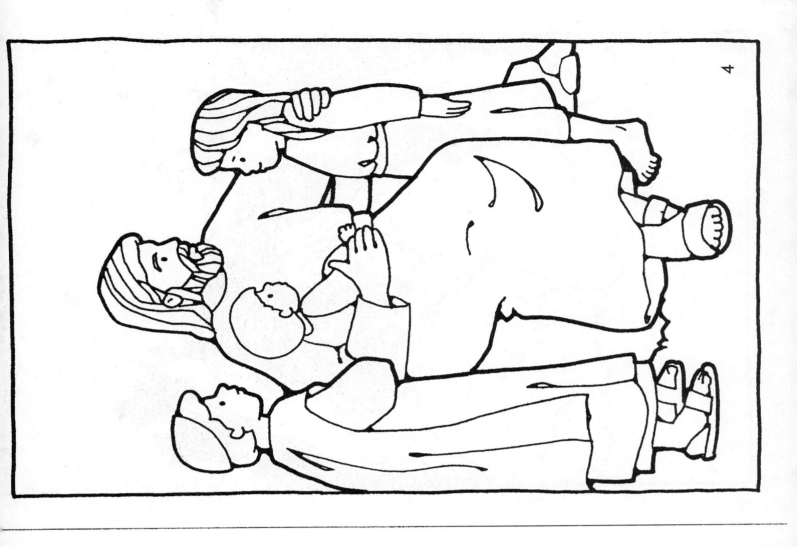

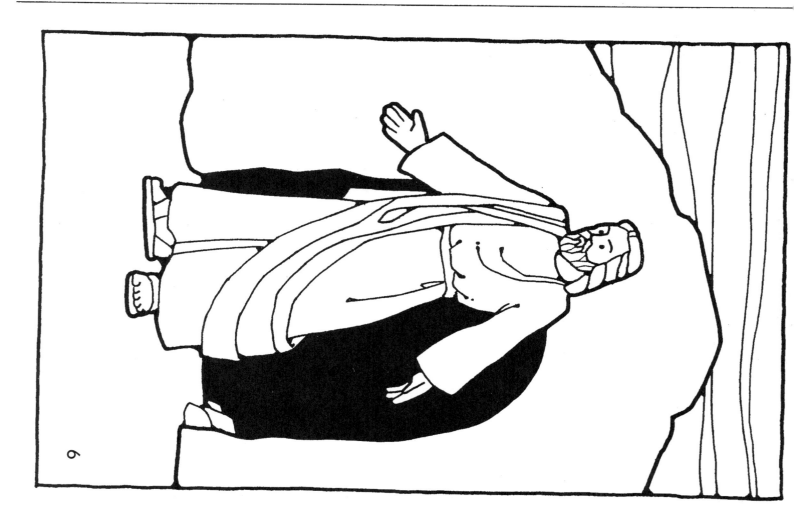

# 2
# Love Is Unconditional

Do good to them that hate you.
(3 Nephi 12:44)

**PREPARATION:** Make two photocopies of the situation cards, one for each participant in the paired acting/speaking parts. If desired, assign the parts the week before the presentation, asking the children to memorize the words or actions. Photocopy enough GOOD and EVIL cards for each child to have one pair. Photocopy and color the picture of Christ's sermon. Glue it to a corner of a poster board. Write the above scripture on the poster and display on an easel. Photocopy the paper doll. (You will need two if you repeat this for sharing time.) Photocopy the television screen and glue it to a box about the same size. Gather the props needed in the situations: a ball, the paper doll, a child's drawing, the pretend television, and two chairs.

**LESSON:** Distribute the GOOD and EVIL cards to the children. Ask, How do you feel about someone who says nice things to you and treats you kindly? You like that person, don't you? It is easy to like people who are doing good to us. How do you feel about someone who tells lies about you, or won't play with you anymore? It is a little harder to like those people, isn't it?

(Point to the picture of Christ.) Jesus taught a wonderful sermon to his followers in Jerusalem. He taught the same message to the Nephites. He said, "Love your enemies, bless them that curse you, do good to them that hate you, and pray for them which despitefully use you, and persecute you" (Matthew 5:44; see also 3 Nephi 12:44). What is Jesus saying? We must try to not return evil for evil. Instead, we must return good for evil.

I have given each of you a card that says "GOOD" and a card that says "EVIL." We are going to observe some situations. I want you to decide if the second person is returning good or evil to the first person. If it is good, hold up the GOOD card. If it is evil, hold up the EVIL card. If it is evil, we are going to repeat what Jesus said, "Do good to them that hate you." (Point to the poster.) Then we will try to think of how the second person could return good instead.

### SITUATION ONE
Person 1 steals ball from Person 2.
Person 2 steals ball back and hits Person 1 on the head with it.

### SITUATION TWO
Person 1 comes into room, tears paper doll, and leaves.
Person 2 comes into room, sees paper doll, and says, furiously: "You jerk! You're not supposed to play in my room! Now look what you've done!"

### SITUATION THREE
Person 1 says: "I don't want to play with you anymore. I have a new best friend."
Person 2 replies: "I feel bad about that. I'll miss you. I still want to play with you."

### SITUATION FOUR
Person 2 holds up his or her drawing.
Person 1 points to the drawing and says: "That's an ugly picture. What's it supposed to be, anyway?"
Person 2 hides the picture and answers: "Nothing your stupid brain would understand."

### SITUATION FIVE
Person 2 accidentally bumps into Person 1.
Person 1 says, angrily: "Hey! Can't you watch where you're going?"
Person 2 says: "Oh, I am so sorry! Did I hurt you?"

### SITUATION SIX
Person 2 is watching television.
Person 1 enters the room, switches the channel, and sits down, saying: "Oh, good, my favorite show is just starting."
Person 2 says: "Excuse me, but I was watching another show. Couldn't we work something out?"

| GOOD | EVIL |
| GOOD | EVIL |
| GOOD | EVIL |
| GOOD | EVIL |

# 3
# Love Is for All

*He inviteth them all to come unto him and partake of his goodness; and he denieth none that come unto him, black and white, bond and free, male and female; and he remembereth the heathen; and all are alike unto God, both Jew and Gentile.*
(2 Nephi 26:33)

**PREPARATION:** Photocopy, color, and cut out the space shuttle and earth. Tape drinking straws to the back of each. Make enough photocopies of the picture of the people for each child to have one. Gather crayons or pencils. For large groups, photocopy the picture onto an overhead transparency and gather an erasable marker and an eraser. Set up the screen and overhead projector.

**LESSON:** Display the picture of the people on the overhead projector, and/or distribute a copy to everyone, along with a crayon or pencil. Have the children follow you in drawing lines around the figures in the picture to demonstrate how we can categorize people according to a number of different characteristics such as age, language, race, or gender. (See diagram.) Then erase the lines (if you are using a transparency), or display a clean copy of the picture. Explain that, where God's love is concerned, there are no differences. God loves us all the same, no matter who we are, what we look like, where we live, or what we do. Even when we disobey him, he still loves us.

(With the space shuttle and earth pictures, make motions to act out a shuttle blasting off and circling the earth. Explain:) Some astronauts once had the opportunity to ride in the space shuttle. One man described how beautiful the earth looked from space; there were no boundary lines, like those we see on maps. He realized that we are all brothers and sisters sharing the same home, the earth.

That is the way God sees us. We are all his children. He does not put us in categories. He loves us all the same. (Read the scripture from the beginning of this chapter, then have everyone repeat, "He inviteth . . . all to come unto him . . . all are alike unto God.") That is the way we should love. We should not think we are better than anyone. We should realize that we are all God's children.

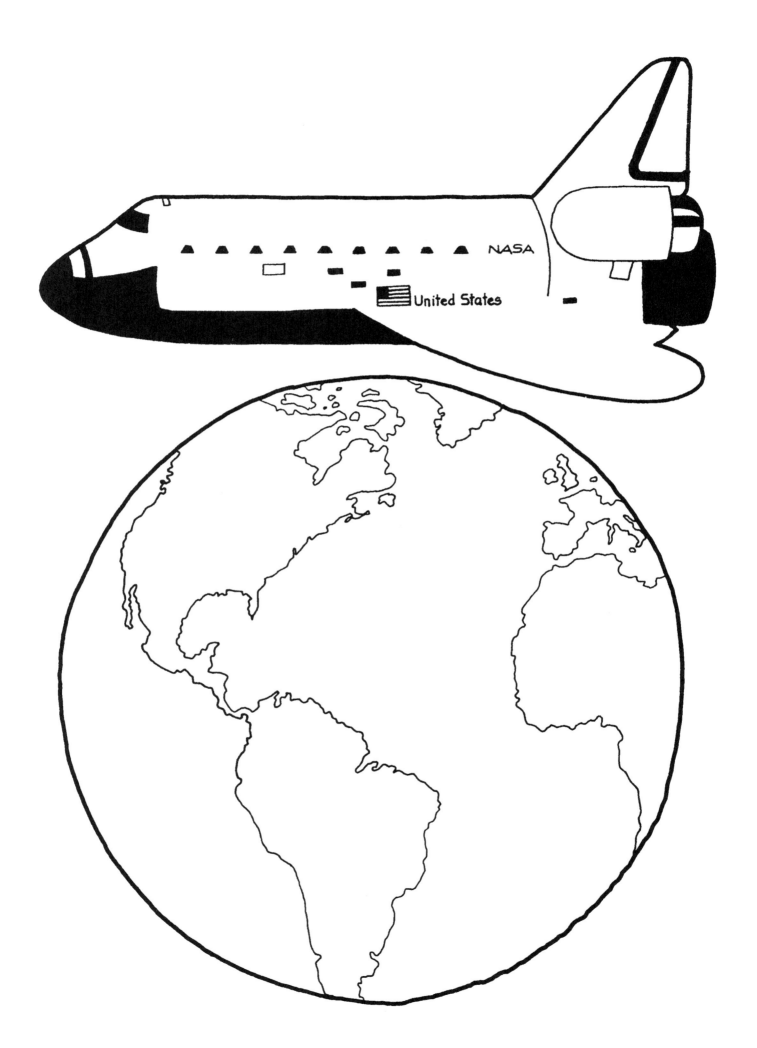

# 4
# Love Does Not Judge Unrighteously

### Judge not, that ye be not judged.
(3 Nephi 14:1)

PREPARATION: Photocopy the rainbow circle, color it, and fold it in half so it looks like a traditional rainbow. Make two photocopies of the script. Glue each to a separate sheet of paper or cloth. Gather three simple Nephite soldier costumes (see diagram), two writing instruments, and masking tape. If desired, ask three boys to practice the dramatization beforehand. Be familiar with Alma 59:1–62:2. Place two chairs in front, one left, one right. Place Moroni's writing instrument under the left chair, Pahoran's under the right.

LESSON: (Hold up the folded rainbow picture.) What is this? Did you know that a rainbow is really a full circle? (Unfold the picture.) From the earth we see only the bow shape. But if we were in the sky looking down, we would see that a rainbow is not just a bow, it is really a whole circle. From the earth, we cannot see the whole picture.

This can happen when we look at people, too. We may think we know all about them. We may decide they are bad. But, as with the rainbow, perhaps we do not have the whole picture. We do not understand everything about other people. We should not judge them. To *judge* people means to decide something about them.

There *are* times when Heavenly Father may need to warn us about someone who might do us harm. If we ever receive a prompting to flee from or avoid someone, we should heed that warning! When we judge by God's spirit, we are judging righteously. But, more often, we tend to make unrighteous judgments using only our own knowledge.

We are going to watch a true example of a time when someone judged incorrectly because he did not have the whole story. (Have three boys dress in the Nephite soldier costumes and act out the following dramatization.)

*MORONI stands on left side. PAHORAN stands on right. SOLDIER enters from left side.*

SOLDIER: Captain Moroni, it is true! The Lamanites have attacked Nephihah and taken the city!

MORONI *(angrily)*: How could this happen? I requested extra troops and provisions from Pahoran. Obviously our governor doesn't care what happens to us out here! But he must care! Without his support, our weary army will be overtaken by the Lamanites.

MORONI *(sits and writes)*: To our governor, Pahoran: You and the other managers of war have neglected us greatly. We have suffered much hunger, exhaustion, and death. It is because of your iniquity that we have suffered. We expect our leaders to strengthen and protect us. But you are lazily sitting on your thrones in Zarahemla! If you do not support us, I will personally come and smite you with my sword! I am Captain Moroni. *(Hands letter to SOLDIER.)* Deliver this at once!

*(SOLDIER delivers letter to PAHORAN, who reads silently, then sits to write his own letter.)*

PAHORAN: Captain Moroni, I am Pahoran, governor of the land. I am sad to know of your great sufferings. I, and all those who love freedom, have been driven out of Zarahemla by some of our own people. They have joined with the Lamanites in controlling Zarahemla. I am not angry because of your letter. I know you did not understand our situation here. I know you love liberty. Join me at once, good captain, and we will both march against evil! *(Hands letter to SOLDIER.)*

Why was Moroni angry with Pahoran? Did Moroni "see the whole picture"? When we are angry with others, it is often because we do not understand their side of the story. That is why Jesus commanded us to "Judge not." (Have everyone recite the scripture, "Judge not, that ye be not judged.")

# 5
# Love Is Humility

Charity . . . is not puffed up. . . . Charity is the pure love of Christ.
(Moroni 7:45, 47)

**PREPARATION:** Photocopy the PUFFED UP and NOT PUFFED UP cards. Photocopy and color both pictures. Mount the pictures on poster board. Gather a balloon, a pin, and a picture of Christ. Cut out the dotted circle in the middle of the picture of the children. Pull the balloon through the hole. Draw a simple face on the end of the balloon, about the same size as the other faces in the picture.

**LESSON:** Carmen's family was on vacation. They decided to ride bicycles built for two people. The bikes were big and heavy. Would Carmen be strong enough to handle one?

Carmen sat on the seat in front of her father. She pushed the pedals down as hard as she could. The bike started to move. Whee! These double bikes were fun! Around and around went her father's feet. Around and around went Carmen's feet. She was so excited! She could do it—she could ride a double bike!

It was hard, steady work to keep the bike going. After they had gone several blocks, Carmen's legs began to get tired. She needed to rest, but she did not want the bike to slow down. Carmen's muscles ached. She breathed harder and harder, almost gasping for air. Exhausted, she finally stopped pedaling.

To Carmen's surprise, the bike kept on going! In fact, it went just as fast as before. All this time, Carmen thought that she was making the bike go. But it was really . . . (Pause for a moment, then ask:) Who was really making the bike go? Yes, Carmen's father.

Sometimes we are like Carmen. Sometimes when we accomplish something, we are very proud of ourselves. We think we did this great thing because we are so smart or so strong. We start to think that we did it by ourselves. We think we don't need people. But we must not forget that others have helped us, and are still helping us, especially our Heavenly Father and our Savior, Jesus Christ.

Have the children repeat the scripture from the beginning of this chapter. Explain that to be puffed up is to think we are better than other people. Demonstrate the process of pride by having children read the PUFFED UP cards. As each card is read, blow the balloon up a little more, until it is full. Tell the children: Eventually, proud people leave no room in their lives for others or for God. They become more vulnerable to Satan's temptations. (Pop the balloon with the pin.)

(Display the picture of Christ. Have children read Christ's sayings on the NOT PUFFED UP cards.) Jesus was not puffed up, because he was full of love. He knew that he needed his Father's help. We should try to be like Jesus.

PUFFED UP cards:

- I have my own room, and you don't.

- I always know the right answers in class.

- Brad's party was really fun. Too bad you missed it!

- Courtney likes me more than you.

- I'm the best soccer player in the league.

NOT PUFFED UP cards:

- John 8:28—Then said Jesus unto them, . . . I do nothing of myself; but as my Father hath taught me.

- John 14:28—My Father is greater than I.

- D&C 19:19—Glory be to the Father.

- Luke 10:21—I thank thee, O Father, Lord of heaven and earth.

- Matthew 11:27—All things are delivered unto me of my Father.

# 6
# Love Is Obedience to God

If ye love me, keep my commandments.
(John 14:15)

PREPARATION: Photocopy, color, and cut out the pictures. Photocopy the TEST OF LOVE cards. Obtain a picture of Christ. Be familiar with Exodus 20 and D&C 89.

LESSON: Sometimes teachers give us tests. The tests show where our knowledge is strong and where it is weak. I am going to give you a test to see how much you know about the way people lived during the time of Christ. (Hold up the paired pictures and ask the questions. For older children you may wish to ask the question first, and delay displaying the pictures until after they have given their answer.)

*Questions*

1. What footwear would Jesus have worn? (Tennis shoe or sandal.)

2. In what setting would Jesus have eaten his meals? (Modern kitchen table or low table with cushions.)

3. What form of transportation might Jesus have used occasionally? (Car or donkey.)

4. What book of scripture records Jesus' life on earth? (New Testament or Pearl of Great Price.)

5. What did Jesus eat in front of his disciples after he was resurrected? (Fish and honeycomb or a frozen dessert.)

That was a test to see how much you *know about* Christ. But what kind of test would tell you how much you *love* Christ?

(Have everyone recite the scripture from the beginning of this chapter while you hold up a picture of Christ.) Jesus, our greatest teacher, tests our love for him by seeing if we will keep his commandments. *He* already knows how much we love him. The tests are for us, to help us know where our love is weak and where it is strong.

(Have children take turns reading the TEST OF LOVE cards. In each situation, determine what commandment is involved and what response would show our love for God.)

**TEST OF LOVE**

Your mother has asked you not to let friends in when she is out. Someone you have been wanting to be friends with is at your door, asking if you can play. Your mother is not home.

**TEST OF LOVE**

Your friend asks you to go to an amusement park with her family this Sunday.

**TEST OF LOVE**

You forgot your lunch money today. You are left alone in your classroom. You see a small pile of coins on someone's desk.

**TEST OF LOVE**

A group of neighborhood children think it is fun to squash caterpillars with rocks. They invite you to join them.

**TEST OF LOVE**

You and a few of your friends from Primary find a pack of cigarettes. One friend suggests that you all smoke them.

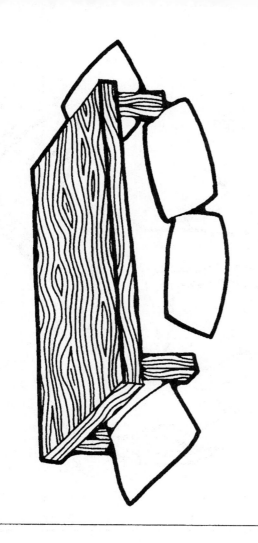
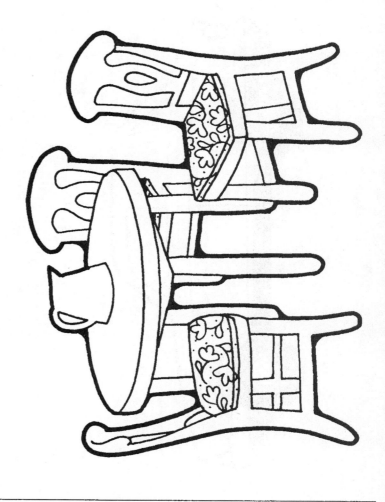
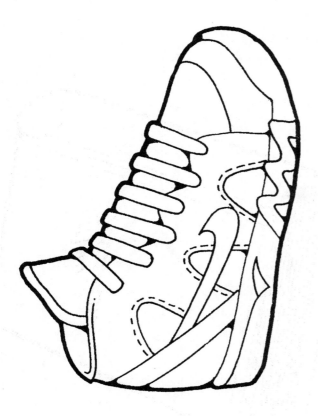
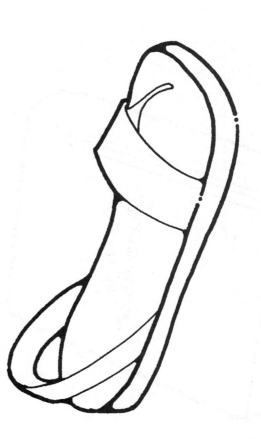

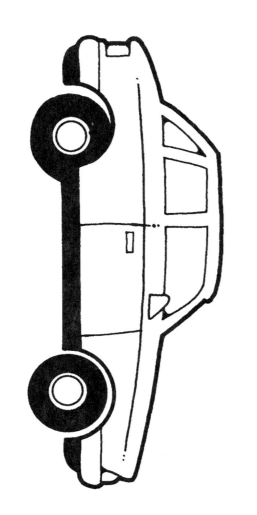

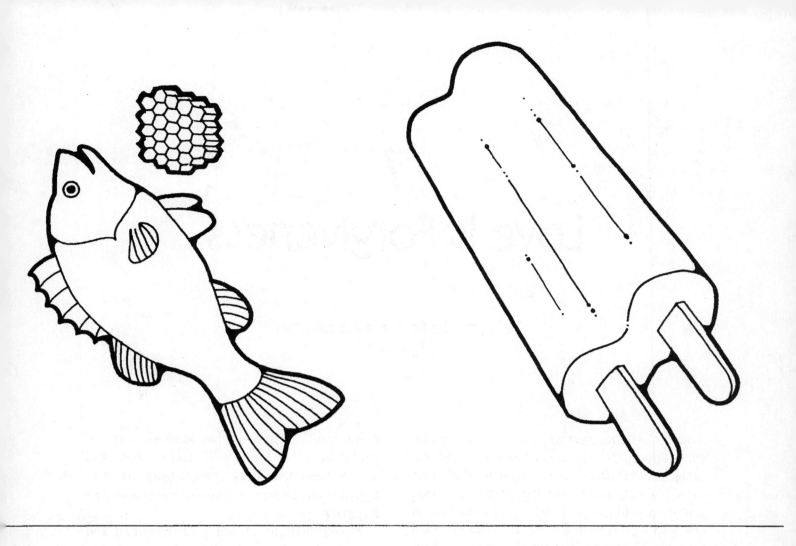

# 7
# Love Is Forgiveness

Ye ought to forgive one another.
(D&C 64:9)

**PREPARATION:** Photocopy and color the picture of Joseph's dream. Gather sheets, pillowcases, and bathrobes to create several ancient Israelite costumes, one Egyptian costume, and a sack of grain. Find a large cardboard box and a picture of Christ. Be familiar with Genesis 37 and 45. Set up the box as a well, and a chair as a throne. Put the grain sack under the chair.

**LESSON:** (Ask a smaller boy to dress up as the biblical Joseph in a beautiful coat. Ask three others to dress as his brothers. Have them act out the following story.)

This is Joseph. He was a good son. He obeyed his father. His father gave him a beautiful coat. Joseph's brothers were jealous. They wished their father did not like Joseph so much. (Joseph pretends to sleep. Hold the dream picture above Joseph's head.) Twice Joseph dreamed that his family was bowing to him. That really made his brothers mad!

One day, when they were away from home herding sheep, the brothers saw Joseph coming. "Here comes the dreamer!" they said to themselves. They were so angry, they wanted to kill him! But instead they stole his coat and threw him into a dry well. Later, they sold him to some travelers. Joseph was taken to Egypt to be a slave. (Have Joseph put on the Egyptian costume.)

The Pharaoh, or king of Egypt, liked Joseph. Joseph could tell the king what his dreams meant. He told the king to save some grain so the people of Egypt would not be hungry. (Joseph holds up the grain sack.) Because of his goodness and wisdom, Joseph became the second most powerful man in Egypt. (Joseph sits on throne.)

Twenty-two years after they had sold Joseph, his brothers came to Egypt, tired and hungry. They did not know that the man on the throne was their brother. They bowed before him and begged for some food.

Joseph was thrilled to see that his family was still alive! He said, "I am Joseph, come near to me. I am your brother, whom you sold into Egypt."

His brothers were surprised and afraid! They had been cruel to Joseph. And now

Joseph had great power. What would Joseph do?

But Joseph said, "Do not be worried, or angry with yourselves. God sent me to Egypt to save your lives." He cried and hugged all his brothers.

What would you have done, if you were Joseph? What should we do when someone is mean to us? (Let the children discuss this. Have the actors remove their costumes and return to their seats.)

(Hold up the picture of Christ.) Jesus said, "Ye ought to forgive one another." (Have the children recite this scripture.) Jesus forgave us, even though we hurt him by sinning. We should try to forgive as Joseph and Jesus did.

# 8
# Love Is Patience

Be patient toward all men.
(1 Thessalonians 5:14)

**PREPARATION:** Photocopy the number dial and mount it on cardboard. Poke a hole in the center. Push a sharpened pencil through the hole. Enlarge the game board if using for a small group, or, for a large group, photocopy the game board onto a transparency and set up an overhead projector. Gather an alarm clock, kitchen timer, or hourglass. Use a button or coin for the game token.

**LESSON:** Today we are going to play a game. But before we can play, we are going to see how patient we can be. I am going to set this timer for two minutes. Let's see if we can sit quietly, without talking, until the buzzer goes off. (Set timer and complete experiment.) It is hard to wait for things that we want, isn't it? But we need to learn how to take turns and be patient.

(Begin the game now. There should be no competition—the whole group moves together, using one token. Have children take turns spinning the number dial like a top. The number that lands flat against the floor or table is the amount of spaces you may move on the board. Follow the directions on the board until the group has reached the goal. Then have everyone recite the scripture, "Be patient toward all men.")

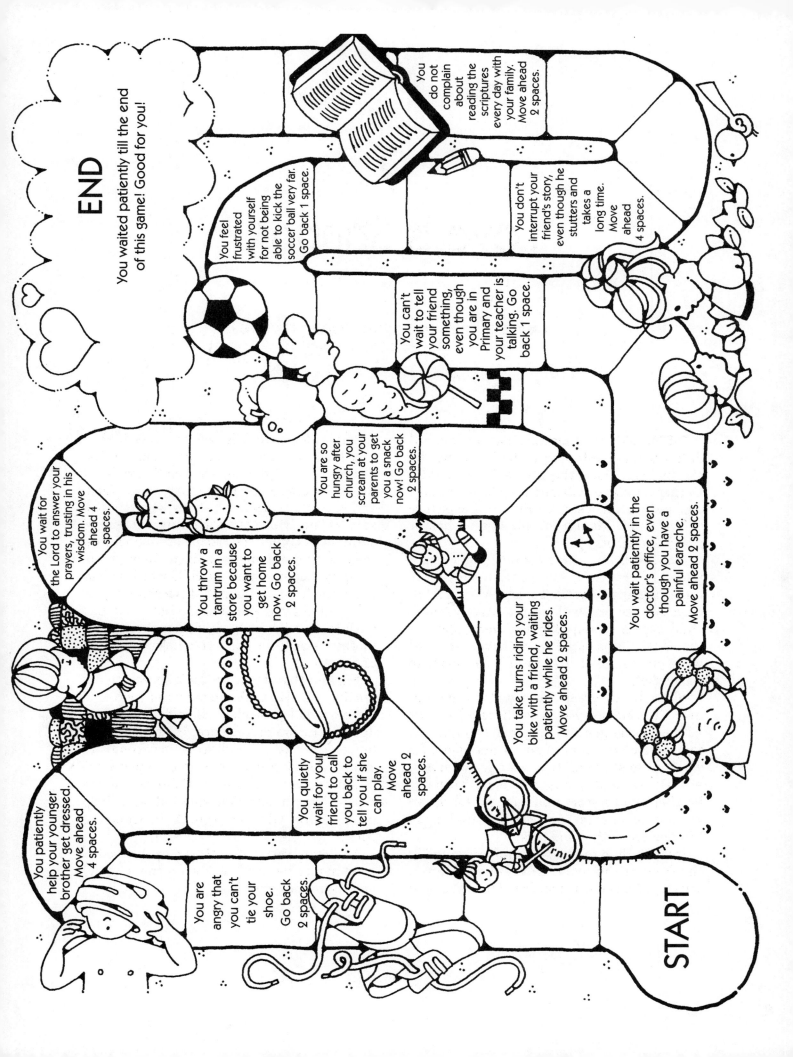

# 9
# Love Is Sharing

It is more blessed to give than to receive.
(Acts 20:35)

PREPARATION: Cut pieces of paper of several different colors into strips, about one inch by six inches. Place the strips in a basket. Gather a picture of Jesus, pencils or crayons, a glue stick, and a stapler. Enlarge the picture of the child. Mount the picture on poster board and display it.

LESSON: Distribute a strip of paper and a pencil or crayon to everyone. Remove any unused strips from the basket. Ask the children to write (you will have to assist younger children) something they love very much on the paper. (For a small group, have each child write on several strips.) Return the strips to the basket.

Show the picture of Jesus, and tell the children: The Savior wants to share all he has with us in the celestial kingdom. He wants us to be equal with him in power and glory. Do we want to share all that we have with others? Do we really want to be equal with our brothers and sisters and friends? Or do we wish to be smarter, or more talented, or to have better clothes and toys?

Invite a child to come forward and stand in the front of the room. Have other children take turns picking a strip from the basket and reading aloud what is written. Ask if they could share that particular item. If the answer is "yes," glue the strip on the poster of the child, creating pants, shirt, shoes, food, and so forth, tearing the strips where necessary. If "no," form the strip into a loop and staple it. As other "no" strips are found, loop them to the first one to make a paper chain. Wrap the chain around the child who is standing in the front. Explain that the chain represents the chain of selfishness. (Note: You may wish to create a demonstration chain prior to the lesson, in case you have few "no" answers.)

Explain that when we don't share, we are hurting ourselves. We are becoming more and more bound by the chain of selfishness. (Use demonstration chain here, if needed.) The longer the chain, the harder it becomes to escape. Selfish people are very unhappy. If we find ourselves bound by selfishness, we can repent. We can ask Heavenly Father to help us to share. (Remove the chain from the child.)

The scriptures tell us, "It is more blessed to give than to receive." (Ask everyone to stand and recite the scripture.)

# 10
# Love Is Sacrifice

I will give up all that I possess. . . . I will give away all my sins.
(Alma 22:15, 18)

PREPARATION: Photocopy, color, and cut out the flannel-board figures. Glue flannel or felt to the backs of the figures. Place a flannel board in front. Obtain a picture of Christ's crucifixion. Be familiar with the principles in Alma 22.

LESSON: How many of you think you love God? Today we are going to talk about sacrifice. To sacrifice means to give something up for God or for others. Sacrifice proves that our love is real.

Listen carefully to this flannel-board story about two sisters. After the story, I want you to tell me what things Mariko decided to sacrifice.

(Use the flannel board and figures to tell the story.)

"I told you to stay off my bed!" yelled Mariko as she pushed Yumi off the upper bunk. "You're never going to use my tape recorder now!"

Yumi started wailing. "Go ahead!" shouted Mariko. "Bawl, so you can get your way again, you little baby!"

"What is going on in here?" asked Mother.

"She pushed me off the bed!" cried Yumi.

"She's not supposed to be up there in the first place!" said Mariko. "I'm sick of her getting into my things."

"Come and help me make dinner, Yumi," said Mother. "Mariko, you had better stay in your room and think about how you've been treating your little sister."

"But Mom, I didn't do anything wrong. It was Yumi!"

That night, Mariko's father called the family together. "Mariko, Yumi, our family has been asked to give contributions to help the earthquake victims," he said. "Many families lost everything. They need food, clothing, and furniture. Your mother and I would like you girls to decide if you have some things you could give. Put the smaller items in this box. I'll deliver them tomorrow."

Yumi ran to her closet. "I have two Sunday dresses. I can put one in the box," she said cheerfully.

Mariko was surprised by Yumi's excitement to share. "Yumi really is a kind girl," she thought. Mariko suddenly felt very sad about the way she had been treating her little sister. The sadness stayed with her all night.

The next morning, Mariko gathered a few dolls and a blanket, and placed them in the box. She was shaking as she took her tape recorder down from the top shelf. "Here, Yumi," she said. "You can play with this. I'm sorry I haven't been very nice to you lately."

Mother walked by and put her arms around the girls. "I am so proud of you two. It isn't always easy to give up our possessions." She squeezed Mariko a little tighter and whispered in her ear, "And it isn't always easy to give up our sins."

What things did Mariko sacrifice? Her possessions (dolls and blanket) and her sin (of being unkind to her little sister). If God asked you to give up your things to help someone who needed them, could you? (Discuss examples. Note that some children will probably get a little worried, thinking that they have to give everything away. Reassure them that they don't have to do that now. But it is worth considering: *If* God were to ask them to sacrifice their possessions, could they?)

If God asked you to give up being unkind, could you? (Discuss other bad habits and wrongdoings they would need to stop.)

(Display the picture of Christ's crucifixion.) Because Jesus loved his Father and us, he was willing to sacrifice everything. If we really love the Lord, we will be willing to give up our sins, as well as anything else the Lord asks of us.

Ask the children to repeat the scripture, "I will give up all that I possess. . . . I will give away all my sins" (Alma 22:15, 18).

# 11
# Prayer Teaches Love

*I have set an example for you. . . . I have prayed unto the Father.*
(3 Nephi 18:16, 24)

PREPARATION: Photocopy and color the pictures. Using the pattern, cut a key out of heavy cardboard. Cover it with foil and tape the word strip, PRAYER, onto it. Following the diagram, cut a small "door" from heavy cardboard. Make a slit the same size as the end of the key, for a "keyhole." Tape a pocket to the back of the door, using construction paper that is slightly larger than the opening. Keeping out the picture of Christ praying, slide the other three pictures into the pocket in numerical order. Be familiar with 3 Nephi 17 and 18.

LESSON: (Hold up the picture of Christ praying for the Nephites.) When Jesus was with the Nephites, he knelt and prayed for the people. The prayer was so beautiful, it could not be written or even fully understood by ordinary people without the help of the Spirit. After the prayer, Jesus blessed all the children. Angels ministered unto them. He told his disciples, "Behold I am the light; I have set an example for you . . . I have prayed unto the Father" (3 Nephi 18:16, 24).

The Son of God set the example for all of us by showing that he needed to pray to his Father. (Hold up the PRAYER key. Use it to open the door, displaying the first picture.) Christ's prayer for the Nephite children opened the door for them to receive blessings and to be administered to by angels.

Everything good comes from God. By ourselves, we cannot really bless others. But if we pray to our Father in heaven in behalf of others, *he* will bless them! According to his will, they will receive what they need. It may be that they would not receive the blessings if it weren't for our prayers.

(Tell the following true stories, using the PRAYER key at the appropriate time to open the door to the corresponding blessing pictures. Or, if desired, substitute true stories about prayer from your own experience, or invite members of your ward or family to share their experiences.)

1. T. J. limped when he got out of bed Christmas morning. Something was wrong with his leg! His mother took him to numerous doctors. X rays revealed a hole in his bone. A disease was eating his bone tissue. T. J. was in a lot of pain. It hurt just to touch his leg! His bishop called for a special fast and prayer. Young and old members of his ward family fasted and prayed to Heavenly Father in behalf of T. J. The day of the fast, the pain lifted. T. J. still needed surgery, but he recovered rapidly. Soon he could walk without crutches.

2. The eleven-year-old Primary girls were

having an activity with their fathers. Amy had been assigned to make the invitations. She was worried. She did not have an idea. She knelt down by her bed and prayed. She asked Heavenly Father to please help her come up with an idea. Then she got ready to go to school. As she was walking to school, an idea came to her. She was able to make a mental picture of the invitation. She knew exactly what to do!

Have the children recite the scripture from the beginning of this chapter. Challenge them to follow Jesus' loving example by praying in behalf of others.

(Note: This chapter was written in response to Elder Jeffrey R. Holland's plea that we teach about the praying Christ. See *A Standard unto My People* [Provo, Utah: Foundation for Ancient Research and Mormon Studies, 1994], pp. 20–21.)

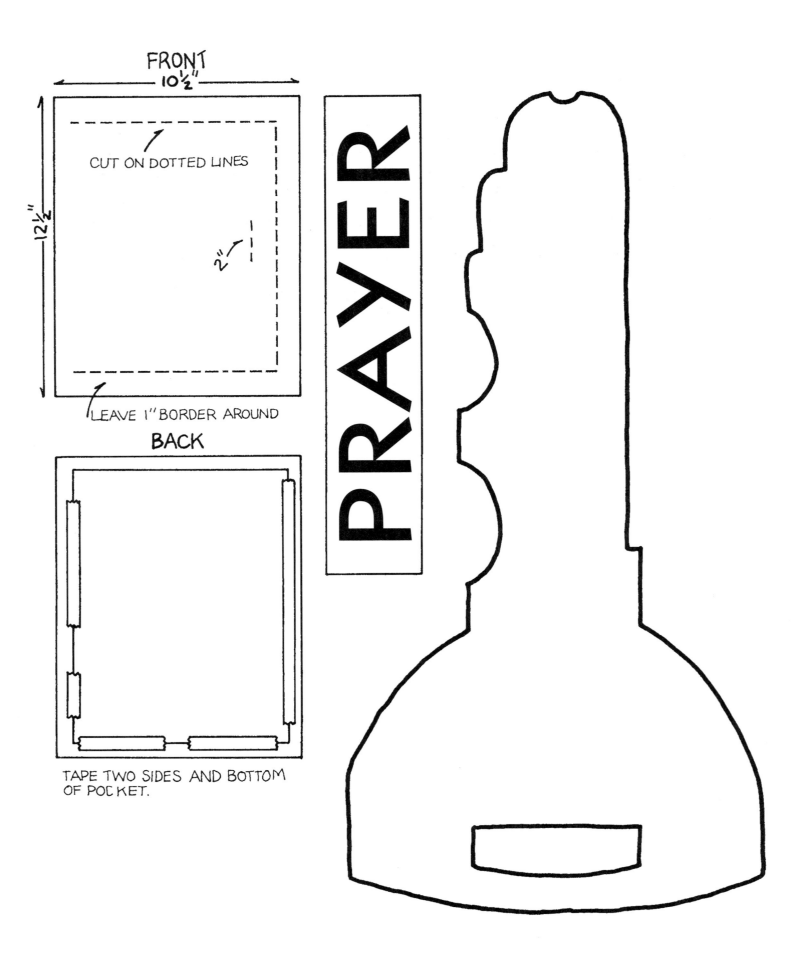

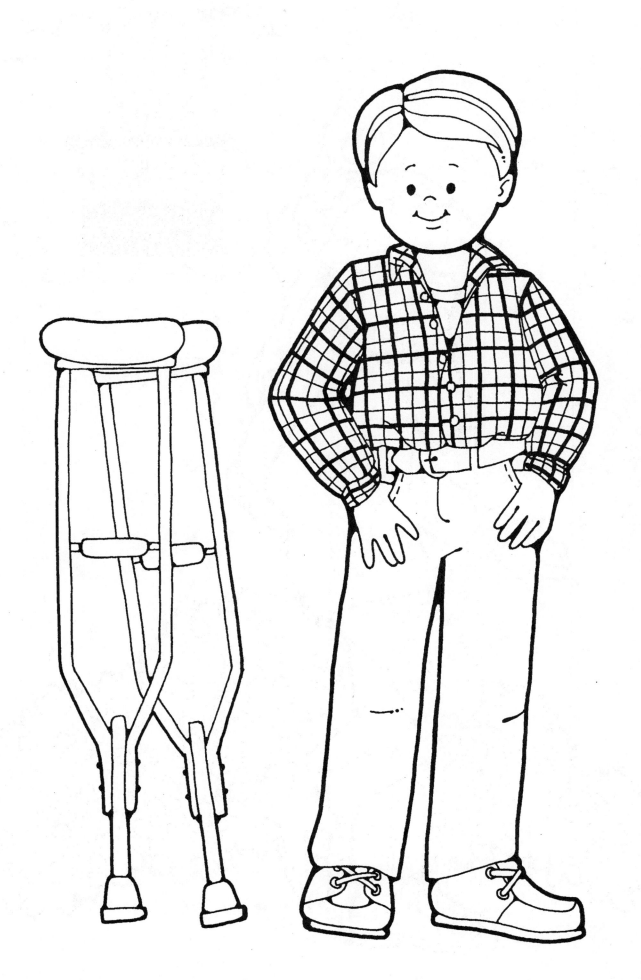

# 12
# The Scriptures Teach Love

Study my word.
(D&C 11:22)

**PREPARATION:** Gather five boxes, baskets, or paper grocery bags. Roll down the tops if you use bags, to make them more secure. Label each one with a book of scripture: Old Testament, New Testament, Book of Mormon, Doctrine and Covenants, and Pearl of Great Price. Put four blank strips of paper and a pen in each bag. Make five copies of the guidelines. Place one in each bag. Gather a lightweight ball, or make one by pulling one sock into another sock, forming a ball shape.

**LESSON:** Divide the children into five groups of mixed ages. Assign each group a book of scripture by giving them one of the labeled bags. Have an adult supervise each group in following these guidelines:

Have everyone return to their regular seats. Set all the boxes or bags in the front with the labels facing the children. The children take turns trying to throw the ball into a bag. (Variation: Lay the bags or boxes on the floor with the openings facing the children, and roll the ball rather than tossing it.) When the ball goes in, the child withdraws a slip from that bag, reads it aloud, and answers the question. The children should not compete in this game, but rather cheer each other on and assist each other in answering when needed.

Emphasize that if we want to know more about the love of Christ, we must study what he has said about it in the scriptures. Have the children recite from D&C 11:22, "Study my word."

### Guidelines
1. Have each member of the group relate his or her favorite story from the assigned book of scripture.
2. Decide which one of those stories to use. Choose one that teaches about love.
3. Review the story together. Look it up in the scriptures.
4. On the paper strips, write four questions or fill-in-the-blank sentences about the scripture story. Place the questions in the bag.

# 13
# The Spirit Prompts Us to Love

**The fruit of the Spirit is love.**
(Galatians 5:22)

PREPARATION: Invite two or three people to share their experiences of being prompted by the Spirit to care for someone. If possible, include one negative example, in which a person was prompted but did not obey, to show the consequences. If you are not aware of any examples, use the true stories at the end of this chapter. Photocopy and color the accompanying pictures.

Cut two pieces of string or yarn, each about ten feet long. Cut two small hearts from red paper and tape one to the end of each string. Gather chalk, eraser, and tape.

LESSON: (Draw a simple tree on the chalkboard.) Does an apple tree produce pears? (Draw pears on the tree.) No, an apple tree produces apples. (Erase the pears and draw apples. Repeat this process two more times, inserting different nuts or fruits into the question.)

Likewise, when we have the Lord's Spirit with us, are we jealous and angry? No. We are patient and gentle, and we want to do good. The fruit of the Spirit is love. (Write THE SPIRIT on the trunk of the tree, and draw hearts as the fruit.) The Spirit of God will always prompt us to act in love. (Have the children recite the scripture from the beginning of this chapter.)

We are not always aware that someone needs our help. We do not always know how to help them. But God knows all things. If we obey his Spirit of love, he will let us know WHEN to help and WHAT to do.

Invite three children to participate in demonstrating this principle. Ask CHILD #1 and CHILD #2 to each hold a heart that is connected to a string. Tape the ends of the strings to the tree on the board. Ask CHILD #3 to sit on the floor and pretend she is learning how to tie her shoe. Have the children act out the following: CHILD #3 is sad because she can not tie her shoe. CHILD #1 is in tune with the Spirit. (Have him keep holding the heart.) He is prompted to teach her how to tie her shoe. CHILD #1 tries to tie, but can not get it right. CHILD #2 is also in tune with the Spirit. She wonders if she should tie CHILD #3's shoes for her. But the Spirit says, "No, encourage her, but let her practice by herself." So CHILD #2 puts her arm around CHILD 3# and says, "You can do it. Don't give up." CHILD #3 finally ties her shoes correctly.

Tell the children that you have invited some people to share their experiences with the Spirit. After the speakers are finished, ask the children to explain the situations back to you. Point out that the promptings were motivated by love. Have the children recite the scripture again.

STORIES:

Six-week-old Matt finally fell asleep on his parents' bed. His mother was very tired, but she knew she had to get breakfast and start the laundry. As she started downstairs, a strong thought came into her mind, "Don't leave Matt on the bed!" But she was so tired, she ignored it. She convinced herself, "He'll be all right. He'll be okay." She went downstairs and started the laundry. The prompting came again, "Go check on Matt!" She raced up to the bedroom and found Matt face down on he bed. She rolled him over. He was blue and barely breathing! Matt had to stay overnight in the hospital.

Telesa was outside playing with her brothers and sisters during a family camping trip. Suddenly she had a strong feeling that something was wrong. As she looked around, she noticed that Tracy, her one-year-old sister, was missing. Where had she wandered? Telesa ran to the trailer, calling, "Mom, Mom! Something is wrong with Tracy!" Mother looked out the window of the trailer and saw Tracy lying face up in the stream!

They hurried to the water and pulled her out. Tracy coughed and started to breathe. They had rescued her in time.

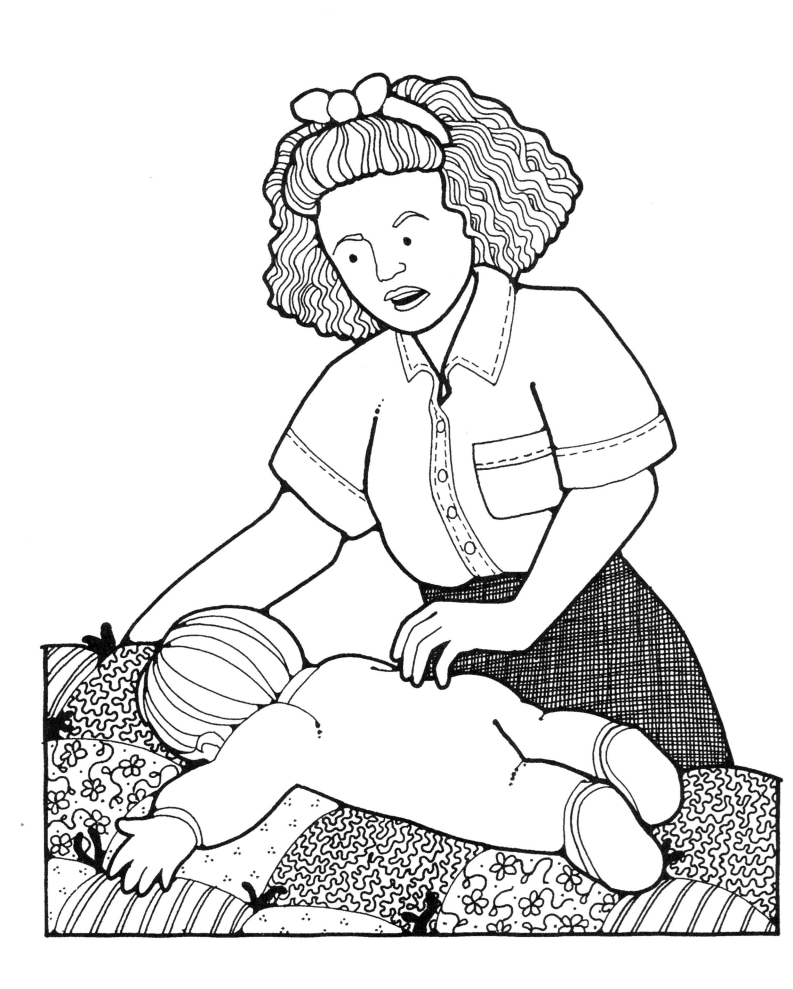

# 14
# Priesthood Ordinances Increase Our Love

Come unto the Father in my name, and in due time receive of his fulness.
(D&C 93:19)

PREPARATION: Obtain a picture of Jesus' baptism. Photocopy the child's baptism picture and the Nephi figure. Put masking tape on the back of the figure. Photocopy enough charts for every child to have one, plus enough small pictures for each child to have a set. If possible, cut out the small pictures beforehand, clipping each set or placing them in small envelopes to distribute to the children. (If time permits, you could have the children cut out their own pictures. Or you might ask some of the older children to help you prepare the pictures a week in advance as part of a class activity.) Gather glue sticks. If your group is not familiar with the song "Baptism" on page 100 of the *Children's Songbook*, print the words out on a poster board. Study 1 Nephi 11:27–33; 2 Nephi 31; D&C 93:11–20.

LESSON: (Display the picture of Jesus' baptism.) We are going to sing a song about when Jesus was baptized. Pay special attention to the second verse, when Jesus tells John the Baptist why he, the Son of God, needed to be baptized. (Sing the song.) Why was Jesus baptized? To fulfill the law, so he could live again with his Father in the celestial kingdom.

John the Baptist saw that Jesus did not receive all of Heavenly Father's power at first. Jesus needed to fulfill all the laws and ordinances of the gospel. Jesus humbled himself to be baptized and receive the Holy Ghost. He received all the ordinances necessary. Then John saw that Jesus received all power from the Father. (See D&C 93:11–20.)

(Tape the Nephi figure lightly to the edge of the picture of Jesus' baptism.) Nephi saw the same thing in a vision. He saw that before Jesus completed his mission on earth, he was baptized and received the Holy Ghost. Before he could suffer for our sins and lay down his life for us, he had to receive power from his Father. (See 1 Nephi 11:27–33.)

(Display the picture of the girl's baptism.) We must follow Jesus' example. If Jesus needed the ordinances of his gospel, how much more must we need them! (See 2 Nephi 31:5–12.) We need the ordinances of the gospel in order to reach our highest potential—to become like Christ and Heavenly Father.

When we obey our covenants, we can be given more and more power until we receive a fullness of power. Our love grows until we have the capacity to love as God does.

(Distribute the charts and small pictures to the children. Have everyone follow along with his or her chart.) This is the way the path to eternal life works. To get on the path, we must be baptized and receive the gift of the Holy Ghost. (Have the children place their baptism pictures on their charts.) When we are baptized, we make covenants—promises to our Heavenly Father—and we take Jesus' name upon us. If we keep the covenants, we increase our capacity to love. We renew our covenants by partaking of the sacrament each week. (Place the smaller sacrament picture.) Then we go through the temple, where we make more covenants. (Place the temple picture.) Again we take Jesus' name on us. If we keep the covenants, we increase our capacity to love. We renew our covenants by partaking of the sacrament. (Place larger sacrament picture.) If we endure to the end, we eventually come back into the presence of God. We have reached our highest potential—to become like Jesus and Heavenly Father. (Place the eternal life picture.)

Who was the first to walk this path? Jesus. He said, "Come unto the Father in my name, and in due time receive of his fulness" (D&C 93:19).

(Distribute glue sticks and have the children glue the pieces onto their charts.)

(For more information, see *A Member's Guide to Temple and Family History Work* [Salt Lake City: The Church of Jesus Christ of Latter-day Saints, 1993], p. 3, and *The Doctrine and Covenants Student Manual* [Salt Lake City: The Church of Jesus Christ of Latter-day Saints, 1981], p. 218.)

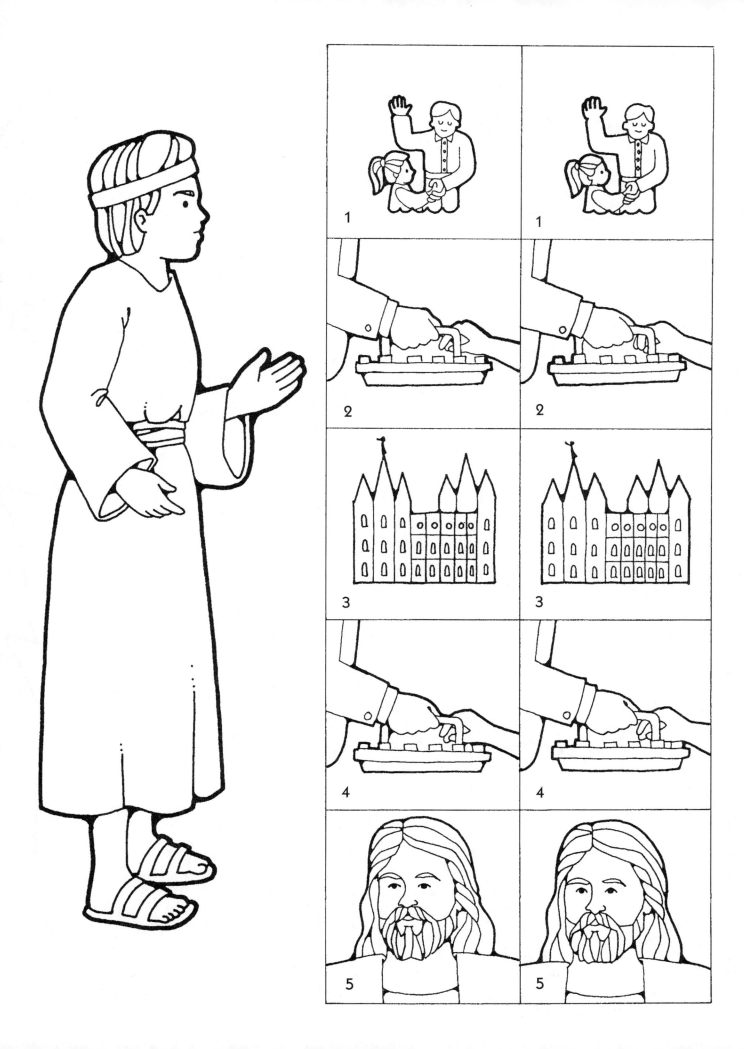

# 15
# Love for Ourselves

Let thy love be for them as for thyself.
(D&C 112:11)

**PREPARATION:** Photocopy (enlarge for a big group), color, and cut out the flannel board figures. Attach masking tape or flannel to the backs of the figures. Gather and display a flannel board.

**LESSON:** (Placing the figures on the flannel board, tell the following true story.)

Eight-year-old Jenae was constantly teased at recess. The children at her new school called her "contaminated." (*Contaminated* means "dirty" or "having germs.") As a game, someone would bump into her and shriek, "Ooo! Now I'm contaminated!" Then that person would touch someone else, to "contaminate" them.

Jenae laughed and pretended not to care. But deep inside, her heart was breaking. "What's wrong with me?" she thought miserably. "It must be these dumb old clothes. And I'm not pretty like the other girls." How she longed for a friend!

One afternoon, Jenae asked her mother to help her with a report for school. She had been too frightened to ask her teacher. But her mother yelled, "Why did you wait until the last minute? Can't you do anything right?"

Head hanging, Jenae went to her room, closed her bedroom door, and started to sob. No one wanted her. Where could she turn now? In the dark silence, she clutched her pillow and asked, "Why was I born, if no one can love me?"

Suddenly a powerful message came into her soul: *"Jesus loves you!"*

*"Jesus loves you!"* With that message came a wonderful feeling of warmth and goodness that filled her whole body. It was like nothing she had ever felt before. She was tingly all over! She sensed that Christ would have liked to hold her in his arms just then. She was at peace.

Jesus' love was so glorious that it left no room for hate in her heart. Jenae thought of the children who had been mean to her at school. But she was not angry. She knew that Jesus loved them, too.

(Ask the children how the story made them feel. Point out that a healthy love for ourselves comes from knowing that no matter what we look like, no matter what we can accomplish, or no matter how many friends we have, God loves us and will always do what is best for us.)

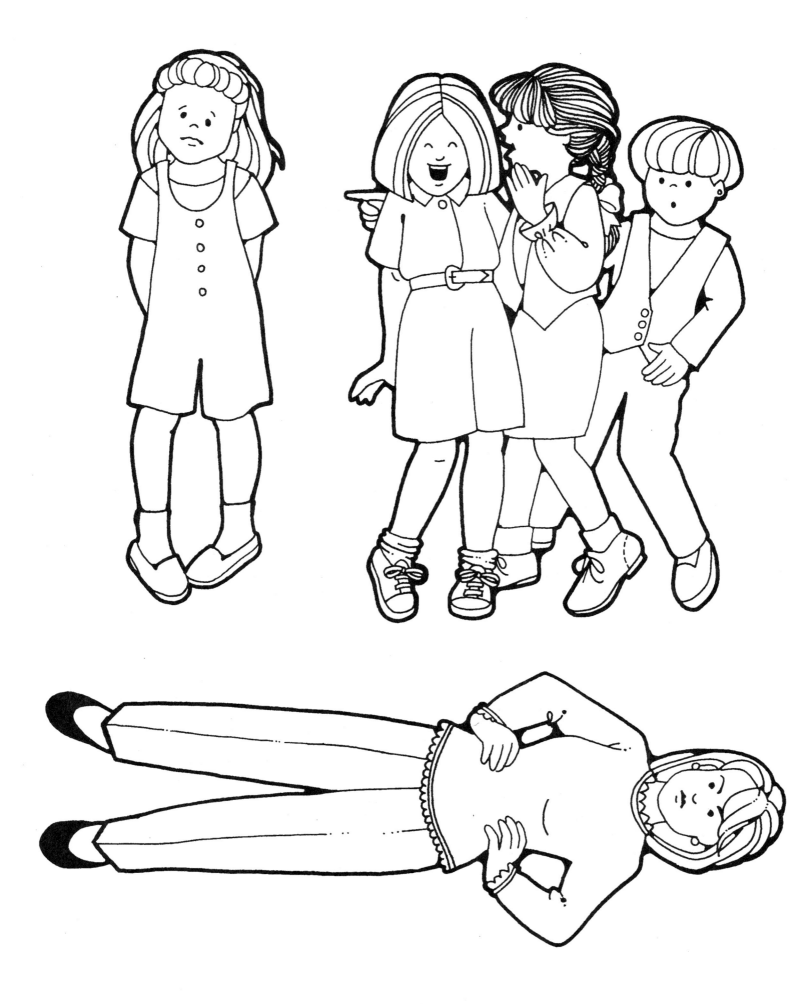

# 16
# Love for Our Families

Thou shalt live together in love.
(D&C 42:45)

PREPARATION: Photocopy (enlarge for a big group), color, and cut out the two homes and their outside flaps. Tape the outer edges of each flap over the rooms by matching the letters. Cut top pictures along dotted lines. (See diagram.) Mount the pictures on heavier board and display. Make and display a banner citing the above scripture.

LESSON: In which of these homes would you like to live? (Let some children choose.) Both places look pretty and peaceful on the outside, but let's see what is happening on the inside. (Allow children to take turns opening the covers, trading off between the two buildings. Discuss the actions inside. Each time a negative scene is depicted, have the children recite the scripture on the banner, then figure out a loving solution to the problem. Repeat this process until all the scenes have been uncovered.) Now, in which home would you like to live? (The one where people love each other.) We should each take the responsibility to fill our homes with love.

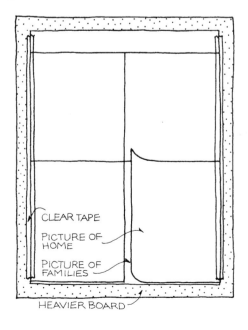

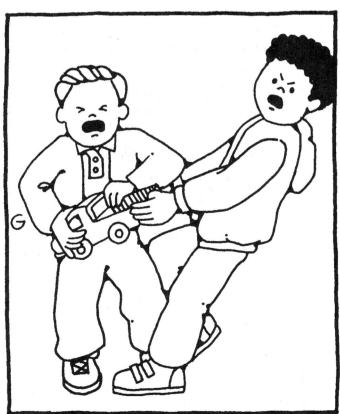

# 17
# Love for Our Friends and Neighbors

Thou shalt love thy neighbour as thyself.
(Matthew 22:39)

PREPARATION: Photocopy and color the pictures of the lamp and King Solomon. Photocopy and cut apart the "How Would You Feel?" cards. Photocopy one figure for each child. Distribute a figure, an extra sheet of blank paper, and a few crayons or markers to each child. Ask the children to fold the blank paper into eight sections. (For young children, you may want to fold the papers beforehand.) Gather masking tape.

LESSON: (Hold up the picture of the Arabian lamp.) President Howard W. Hunter said, "If you could have one wish, what would it be?" (Allow some children to respond.) President Hunter continued, "There are so many things we wish for as we go through life. . . . Nearly every child who has read the story of the *Arabian Nights* has wished for a lamp like the one Aladdin had, which when rubbed would summon the genie who would do the bidding regardless of the request made of him."

A long time ago, the Lord told King Solomon he could have anything he wanted. King Solomon could have asked for money, or protection from his enemies, or a long life. Out of all the things he could have asked for, he pleased the Lord by asking for a spiritual gift: an understanding heart. Why do you think the Lord was pleased that Solomon asked for an understanding heart? (Because it showed that Solomon cared about other people and wanted to obey God's commandments.)

(The two preceding paragraphs are based on Howard W. Hunter, *That We Might Have Joy* [Salt Lake City: Deseret Book Company, 1994], pp. 186–90.)

If we care about people, we will try to understand the way they feel. We will obey God's commandment (have the children recite with you): "Thou shalt love thy neighbour as thyself."

(Play the "How Would You Feel?" game. Have the children take turns reading aloud the situations on the cards. After each card is read, all the children should draw a happy or sad face in one of the sections of their blank paper, showing how they would feel if that situation happened to them.)

What if we all asked the Lord for an understanding heart, as Solomon did? What if we obeyed the Lord's commandments by always treating our friends and neighbors the way we would like to be treated?

(Have the children color the figures to depict themselves with happy, understanding hearts. Make a mural by taping the figures next to one another around the room. Recite the scripture again.)

**How Would You Feel?**

Your picture was chosen to decorate the cover of the school program. But your friend seems upset and says, "I don't care about your dumb picture."

---

**How Would You Feel?**

You forgot to bring your lunch to a field trip. Your classmate says, "Don't worry, you can have half of mine."

---

**How Would You Feel?**

You look out your window and see a boy taking your bouncy ball to his yard. He did not ask if he could take it.

---

**How Would You Feel?**

You have a broken leg and cannot play for a while. A neighbor comes to keep you company. (Draw the picture for the second sentence.)

---

**How Would You Feel?**

Your friend puts an arm around you and says, "You're my friend."

---

**How Would You Feel?**

You find out that one of your friends has been saying unkind things about you.

---

**How Would You Feel?**

You just fell out of a swing. Another child laughs and says, "You look so funny!"

---

**How Would You Feel?**

Someone in your Primary class says, "We missed you last week."

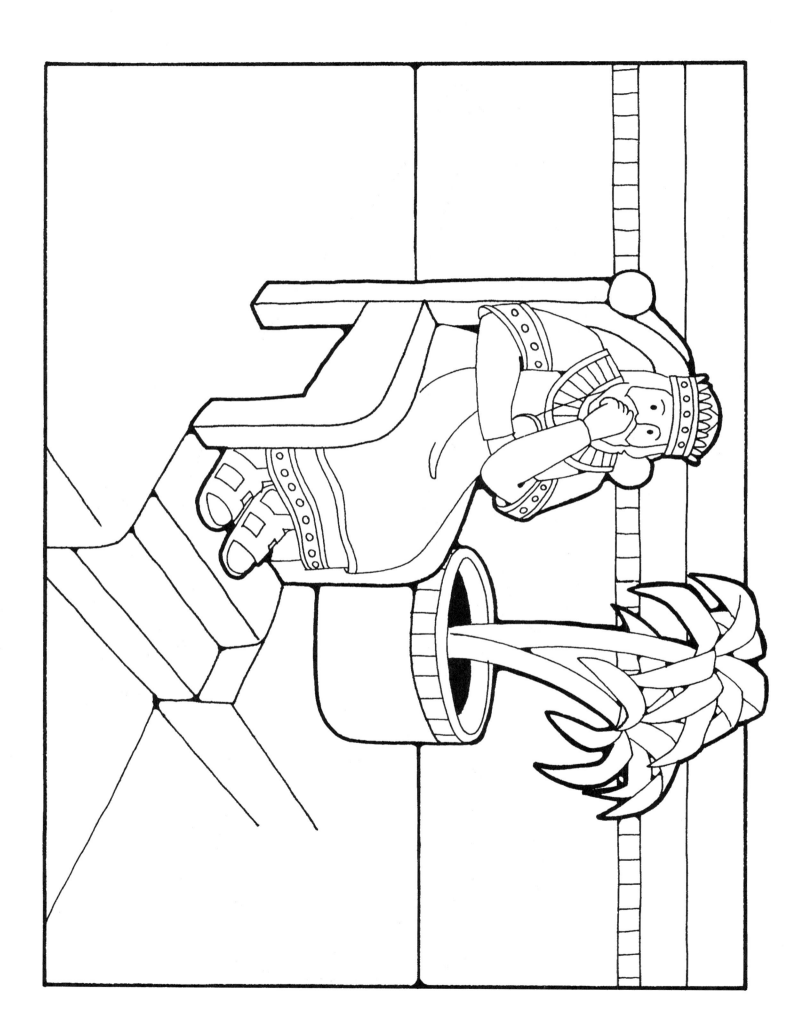

# 18
# Love for the Whole World

Whosover drinketh of the water that I shall give him shall never thirst.
(John 4:14)

PREPARATION: Photocopy a missionary grid for each child. If desired, obtain a picture of President James E. Faust and tape a copy of his quotation lightly on the back. Gather nine place markers for each child. These could be cut out of paper or cardboard, or, if the situation allows, use miniature marshmallows or candies as markers. Bring a cracker and a paper cup for each person. Fill a container with ice water. Be familiar with the scripture references in this chapter.

LESSON: (Give everyone a cracker to eat, to cause their mouths to feel dry.) I want all of you to imagine that you are wandering in a hot, dry desert. You have not had anything to drink for two days. Warm winds throw sand against your blistering body. All you can think of is water, *water,* WATER! If only you could have a sip of cool, refreshing water! Then a traveler comes near and tells you where you can find water. You find the well. (Distribute cups of water to all and let them drink.) Ah! Doesn't that renew your spirits? Doesn't that satisfy your thirst? Wouldn't you be grateful to that traveler for sharing his knowledge with you?

Many people throughout the world are like wanderers in a desert that offers no satisfaction. They are terribly thirsty for the spiritual water that can come only from Jesus Christ. (Hold up the picture of President Faust.) President James E. Faust said, "What can we do for the peoples of the earth? What can we give that no one else can? . . . The answer is simple. We can offer the hope promised by the Savior. . . . [We can] teach God's children everywhere to accept and keep the commandments of God. . . . He that partakes of this water, as the Savior said, 'shall never thirst'" (*Ensign,* May 1995, p. 62).

(Have the children recite the scripture from the beginning of this chapter. Ask them what it means. Clarify that people get thirsty spiritually as well as physically. If we are good examples, and are willing to share our testimonies of the gospel of Jesus Christ, others might turn to Christ and quench their spiritual thirst.)

We have many examples of good people who led others to the spiritual waters of Christ. We are going to play "Fill in the Grid." When a description is read, find the corresponding picture and cover it with a marker. (Distribute grids and place markers. Older children could take turns reading the descriptions. Younger children should be assisted, so that all the children complete their grids together. If the markers are edible, invite the children to eat them after the game.)

DESCRIPTIONS:

1. This man ate locusts and honey while he lived in the desert. He prepared the way for

Jesus by preaching repentance and baptizing with water. (John the Baptist—Matthew 3.)

2. This person told a Samaritan woman at a well, "Whosoever drinketh of this water shall thirst again: But whosoever drinketh of the water that I shall give him shall never thirst." (Jesus Christ—John 4:13–14.)

3. This missionary taught the poor Zoramites that the word of God is like a seed that must be planted in our hearts. (Alma—Alma 32.)

4. This holy being taught Adam and Eve about the sacrifice of the Savior. (An angel—Moses 5:6–8.)

5. These men had no money. Many of their wives and children were sick. Yet they left their families to preach the gospel in England. Thousands joined the Church because of their efforts. (The early Latter-day Saint missionaries—see *Doctrine and Covenants Stories* [Salt Lake City: The Church of Jesus Christ of Latter-day Saints, 1983], pp. 180–81.)

6. Megan's friend asked her why she was so happy. Megan said, "I guess it's because I know that God loves me. He hears my prayers. I want to know him better." (Modern girl.)

7. God asked this man to preach the gospel of repentance to the people in Nineveh. The man was afraid. He tried to run away, but ended up being swallowed by a huge fish. The fish spit him out. Then he preached in Nineveh, and the people did repent! (Jonah—Jonah 1–3.)

8. These two men were thrown into prison for preaching the gospel and casting out evil spirits. After miraculously escaping, they converted the prison guard. (Paul and Silas—Acts 16.)

9. These four brothers each gave up the chance to be king. Instead, they wanted to preach the gospel to the Lamanites. (Ammon, Aaron, Omner, and Himni, the sons of King Mosiah—Mosiah 28:1–10.)